CREATE

**AN INTENSIVE BIZ PLAYBOOK &
PLANNER FOR DIGITAL SOLOPRENEURS**

CONTENTS

Before we dive in, go to **CREATEPLANNER.COM/PLAYBOOK-BONUS**
to download the bonuses that go together with this book.

I'm convinced that about half of what separates the successful entrepreneurs from the non-successful ones is pure perseverance.

STEVE JOBS

———————

Cofounder and CEO of Apple

LET'S BUILD A BUSINESS YOU CRAVE

What month is it right now?

What part of the business season is this for you?

Did you just wind down March which is crunch time for your business?

Or is it inching toward December, and you're feeling all that pressure to take stock for next year?

Whatever month or time of the year you pick up a copy of this workbook, it doesn't matter. There is nothing earth-shattering about December or January that makes it red hot and prime to take stock and set goals. The date is largely immaterial. It's just the significance that we give to it as business owners. You're not behind. There's no catching up needed.

You are right where you need to be to build a business you crave.

I remember sitting in my room in May this year looking at what I had sketched out in November the previous year: my ideas for new offers; marketing assets I wanted to create; new directions I wanted to explore; past campaigns I wanted to rerun.

Many had me at "What were you thinking?"

> You have to let the roots spread out and entrench themselves in the soil. The more you let it grow, the more it produces.

Several of these ideas I had crossed off the list just three months into the new year. The others that I did indeed work on were an amalgamation of a few different ideas. The ones that stuck and grew strength to strength were the battle-tested campaigns that I had run. These were the ones that weren't perfect the first or second time I ran them but that I stuck with, tested, and tweaked. That's not to say that old ideas are gold and new ones fail. But if you want something to bear results, you have to let it grow.

You have to let the roots spread out and entrench themselves in the soil. The more you let it grow, the more it produces. So give your campaigns, assets, and offers time to grow and develop. Give them a chance. Reflect and reframe them by all means but see where they take you before giving up.

As a business owner, that's the trap we often fall into. We start a new business when we lose momentum for another, or when sales tank. We switch focus to creating new offers when our current ones aren't getting us the results we're looking for. We fall into repeated feast or famine cycles of revenue highs and lows.

Yet, we don't reflect on what got us there in the first place. What is it about the foundation or the roots or the soil that needs to be changed so that you get different results? A good farmer knows that no matter how many new plants he sows, the results are going to be the same if he doesn't change what he can't see—what's beneath the ground.

That's what this planner or business workbook helps you do. It helps you reflect, reframe, and realign different aspects of your business before you make space for completely new opportunities. The questions in this book are not the typical questions raised in other business planners. You will not just find "How much did this product make this year?" or "How much did you grow your community?" type of questions.

You will dig deeper.

It may require work on your part especially if you're not attuned to what's going on with your business. It may get uncomfortable because this playbook may leave you with more questions than answers.

I want to assure you that questions are a good thing.

Questions mean that you are opening your mind to the possibilities. But I promise you that the questions raised will shed a whole new light on your business and where you need to go. You will also be presented with prompts and suggestions every step of the way. Think of it as an exercise with your business coach. Because only when you consider the tough questions will you be able to design a business that embraces your **zone of genius.**

Why is this important?

Because you attract your ideal customers when you operate in your zone of genius. This is what your ideal customer is buying into. This is when your business is tailor-made for you and isn't modeled after anyone else's. If you've ever wondered why following someone's advice hasn't worked for you when it's been able to give several others amazing results, this is why.

You best serve your zone of genius when your brand, offers, and business model + revenue strategies are aligned. That's exactly what we want to do here.

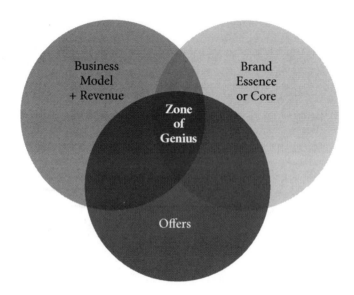

One of my favorite quotes is by Jeff Ernst, a former analyst at Forrester Research: "Business buyers don't 'buy' your product or service; they 'buy into' your perspective and approach to solving their problems."[1] The real competitive advantage of a business today is not the optimized landing pages, emails, or even content for that matter.

It's the trust you build with people. It's the authority you have over your niche or topic. It's your zone of genius. Now, that cannot be copied or replicated. Because it's tied to how subscribers and customers experience your brand.

Are you operating in your zone of genius? Let's find out.

Take the Biz Zone of Genius Quiz here: **createplanner.com/biz-quiz**

HOW THE PLANNER IS STRUCTURED

The planner is structured into seven different business areas:

Your
Vision

Your Zone of
Genius

Your
Marketing Mix

Your Digital
Presence

Your Offers (Products
& Services)

Your Revenue &
Income Plan

Your
Goals

In each area, you will follow a four-part process:

Review (Where you are and what's already working) – **Analyze** (Where you need to be) – **Reframe and Realign** (Where you need to go) – **Act** (What can you do today and what steps you need to take to make the biggest impact)

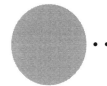

Where you are

Where you need to be

Where you need to go

Why is it done this way?

Like I mentioned at the beginning, you can't replicate your success or know where your business needs to go unless you review and analyze what your current state is. You need to look beneath the surface to see what's working and what isn't because you can't solve a problem you don't know exists.

CONCEPTS AND TERMS INTRODUCED IN THE CREATE BUSINESS PLAYBOOK AND PLANNER

MARKETING

Can we discuss your business without discussing marketing?

No.

But what exactly does marketing encompass?

Selling?

Promotion?

Advertising?

Marketing isn't just about selling or promotion. It's also about attracting and capturing your ideal customers. In a nutshell, marketing is made up of these four activities:

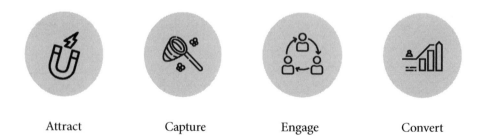

| Attract | Capture | Engage | Convert |

Have a look at the diagram below. This encapsulates what a marketing system would look like for your business.

The seven areas – Your Vision – Your Zone of Genius – Your Marketing Mix – Your Digital Presence – Your Offers (Products & Services) – Your Revenue & Income Plan – Your Goals – are cogs that fit into your marketing system. If they don't function well, your system does not serve optimally. We will refer to this diagram throughout the playbook to see how areas of your business fare with regard to this system.

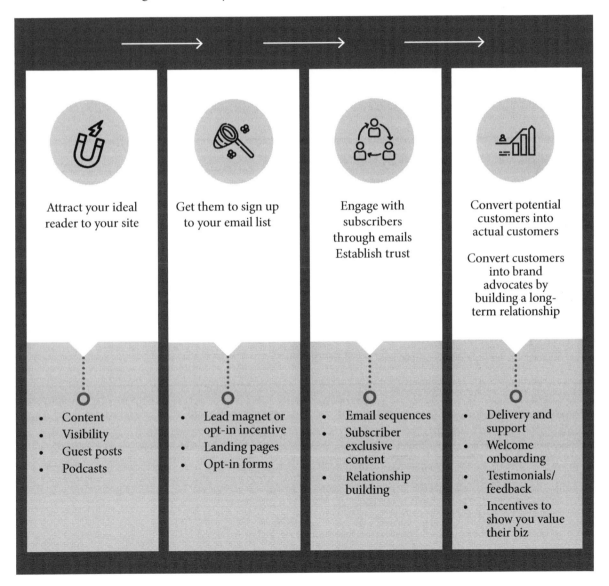

MARKETING ASSETS

Marketing assets are elements that are used to help carry out each of the activities on page 11.

Examples of marketing assets are

Challenges	Emails	Quizzes
Videos	Audio recordings	Checklists
Cheat sheets	White papers	

These help you move your ideal buyer or customer along the following phases: stranger > reader > subscriber > engaged subscriber > customer > brand advocate

IDEAL BUYER or CUSTOMER
You will see the terms ideal buyer or customer used throughout this workbook rather than the terms target market or target audience.

Why?

Target audience provides a broad summary of the people you are marketing to. It usually gives an average demographic profile by lumping together age, gender, marital status, income, and location into a whole.

An example would be: Female, 23–40, mom, moderate income, living in the USA

Ideal buyer or customer personas are more detailed and unique than target audience profiles. These refer to people you want to actively market to.

For instance, my ideal buyer is a twenty-seven-year-old female. She is likely to be a mother of two kids and is looking to start a business from home. But she is not someone who identifies or relates to the term mom blogger or mompreneur. She sees herself as a solopreneur or small business owner. She is likely to have money mindset issues as well as imposter syndrome. She often wonders who the heck she is to call herself an expert. Her main issue is time because she juggles her family and kids as well. She is not someone who shies away from hard work and she takes action. She is unlikely to be someone who purchases a course and never gets to it. She sees herself as a simple person. Jeans and a simple top are her staples. She knows she needs to invest in herself to start her business, and she doesn't believe that free is best.

An ideal buyer is someone who you love to work with and serve. Knowing who these people are in your business will help you make better decisions about your offer which includes the promises or outcomes, how you package it, pricing, as well as the language you use on your sales page.

As a solopreneur and small business owner, you don't have the capacity to target many different customer segments unlike huge brands like Procter & Gamble or Unilever who may have ten or more customer segments for each product they have on offer. Hence, it's ideal to focus on 1–2 segments at most so that you can speak the right language to the right customer since each segment will have different triggers that make them buy.

Note: I go into detail on how to craft your ideal buyer personas in my other two books *The One Hour Content Plan* (1hcp.me) and *Your First 100* (yourfirst100.com).

A **negative persona** is someone who you don't want to market to because they are not your ideal buyer. This is a description of behaviors and possibly demographics of who you want to exclude from your buying pool. I have a sprinkling of who my negative persona is within the paragraph above.

Maybe you're thinking: *Why would I want to do that? Isn't a buyer still a buyer?*

Well, because these are the people who are least likely to get results from your offers. They are also least likely to gel with your style. They may also account for higher refunds and returns.

Take a few minutes now to quickly write a paragraph on who your ideal buyer is. Refer to the questions and prompts below to see what you need to include. You also want to craft a description of your negative persona.

Prompts

- Gender
- Where they live
- Age
- Occupation
- Marital Status
- His/her desired outcomes are (try to rank in order of the most important outcomes to the least)
- His/her pain points are (try to rank in order of greatest pain)
- What interests/hobbies does he/she have?
- Where does he/she hang out on social media?
- What does he/she believe is stopping him/her?
- What does he/she despise?

IDEAL BUYER 1

IDEAL BUYER 2 (SKIP IF NECESSARY)

CREATE An Intensive Biz Playbook & Planner For Solopreneurs

Negative Persona

(Prompt: If you're having difficulty with this, use the following statement prompts to craft a negative persona: My ideal customer is unlikely to see herself as…view herself as…My ideal customer is unlikely to do…My ideal customer is unlikely to think that…My ideal customer does not use the words…)

With this foundation in place, you're equipped with everything you need to make the best use of this workbook. Share your progress with me on social media @meerakothand.

Let's go!

YOUR VISION

"

For all of the most important things, the timing always sucks. Waiting for a good time to quit your job? The stars will never align and the traffic lights of life will never all be green at the same time.

The universe doesn't conspire against you, but it doesn't go out of its way to line up the pins either. Conditions are never perfect. 'Someday' is a disease that will take your dreams to the grave with you. Pro and con lists are just as bad. If it's important to you and you want to do it 'eventually,' just do it and correct course along the way.

TIMOTHY FERRISS

Author of The 4-Hour Workweek

Ever wondered why every goal-setting exercise starts with vision?

Maybe you secretly think that it's all fluff. How can a lofty picture of what you imagine will happen in three or five years be important to the present? How is it important in driving action? I'll tell you why you should take the power of having a vision seriously.

A part of us is wired to avoid uncertainty. Call it carried over survival instincts from the caveman days. This is baked in science where researchers have found that a part of the brain—the amygdala—reacts negatively when we are faced with change or uncertainty. In the book *The War of Art*, Steven Pressfield calls this our lizard brain.[2] The brain that wants to maintain the status quo…that wants to preserve what you have now because it's scared of change, trying out new things, or taking risks.

But the good news is that you can overcome this with a compelling vision. The brain (nerdy version: the prefrontal cortex) lights up when you're excited about a compelling outcome or vision. A clearly defined vision keeps you moving even if you're fearful of change or uncertainty. It stops you from being stuck and helps you make those hard decisions that you wouldn't otherwise have made because your instincts didn't want to "rock the boat."

But here are common pitfalls people make when coming up with a vision:

The danger in modeling a vision or business model set by someone else is that it's tailor- made to fit them, not YOU

1. Your vision isn't bigger than your present. Without a compelling vision, you may find that you have no reason to go through pain, change, or feel motivated to choose discomfort over comfort or to overcome challenges and fears.

2. The vision is not yours and instead is what people say it should be. We've been taught that growing our business has to equate to hiring employees, growing a team, having an of-fice space, and outsourcing everything other than approvals. This may be the perfect greater vision for someone else but not necessarily for you. Is the vision you create what you want or what people say it should be?

3. Your business vision is at odds with your vision for your life.
   My friend Cath is a Pinterest manager and has a calendar full of clients. She loves offering

one-on-one services and the comfort of working from home. She loves the freedom of being there to take care of her son's needs. She doesn't crave growing into an agency or hiring four other Pinterest managers though that may be what others aspire to do.

Does not wanting this "greater vision" mean you're unmotivated?

No, it doesn't. It means that you know what you want from your business. You know what works best for the life you want. So if your vision doesn't fit what you think is the "right" vision, that's fine. But if your vision is at odds with how you want to live your life, you have some serious reflection to do to start being honest about what you really want .

Will this change? Maybe.

You may find yourself longing for something that you may not have thought of three years earlier. You may feel the sudden hunger for new business branches you never thought of. But no matter how your vision for your life changes, your business vision has to complement that. The danger in modeling a vision or business model set by someone else—even the most successful people—is that it's tailor-made to fit them, not YOU. So you may find yourself following someone successful but still failing because you're ne-glecting what's important to you and where you shine.

In this section, you will define a vision that's meaningful to you. Your vision will help you define your goals for the next twelve months and how these translate into the four quarters.

What worked really well for your business last year?

What goals didn't you reach last year?

What challenges did you face?

CREATE An Intensive Biz Playbook & Planner For Solopreneurs

Where do you see yourself in three years?

Create a personal vision that captures and articulates what you want for your **LIFE** in three years.

What level of security do you seek?

What level of income and fulfillment do you want?

What do you really want to do with the time you have?

What do you want for yourself and your family?

What legacy do you want to create?

Where do you see your BUSINESS in three years?

Create a personal vision that captures and articulates what you want for your **BUSINESS** in three years.

Where do you see your LIFE in one year?

Create a personal vision that captures and articulates what you want for your life in one year.

Where do you see your BUSINESS in one year?

Create a personal vision that captures and articulates what you want for your business in one year.

What do YOU need to become to achieve this vision?

E.g., I read at least two books every month; I wake up an hour earlier to write my goals down every day; I am part of a master-mind group of peers that surrounds and supports me.

What does your BRAND need to BECOME to achieve this vision?

YOUR VISION SPACE

Definition: A vision board is a tool used to help clarify, concentrate and maintain focus on a specific life goal. Literally, a vision board is any sort of board on which you display images that represent whatever you want to be, do or have in your life.

YOUR ZONE
OF GENIUS

Your brand isn't what you say it is; it's what your customers experience and tell others. You can craft a professional image, dress it up in expensive design, and send it out into the world, but if it comes with stories that don't match, the stories will win every single time.

SCOTT STRATTEN & ALISON KRAMER

Unselling

What does operating in your zone of genius mean? It means

1. Picking your specialty and focusing on finding ideal customers who need help in that area. By addressing unique concerns in that area and showing that you're willing to learn more about it, you position yourself as a thought leader or expert.

2. Regularly offering insights about that area or speciality. You stand for something and aren't afraid of sharing it even if it goes against the grain. You have a point of view.

3. Being aware of what helps you attract your ideal customer and what sets you apart from others in the same niche as yours. What are people drawn toward with you and your brand? The way you write? The type of videos you create? Your insightful audio commentary? Do more of that.

What operating in your zone of genius doesn't mean?

Staying in your comfort zone.

When you operate in your zone of genius you

1. Set yourself apart from others in the industry even if you offer similar products and services. There's no way your audience can confuse you with anyone else because you clearly stand out.

> When you operate in your zone of genius you set yourself apart from others in the industry even if you offer similar products and services

2. Have loyal customers who buy from you repeatedly.

3. Enjoy word of mouth marketing. Your engaged subscribers and brand advocates willingly spread the word about you and your business. This attracts new business opportunities to you.

Now ask yourself if you can say yes to all three of these statements above?

If you can't, it's time to reflect and rethink the brand you've built. If you've read my books Your First 100 and The One Hour Content Plan, you know the power of a personal brand. A brand is a set of emotions that your audience attaches to you. In his book The Brand You 50,[4] Tom Peters describes a brand as a promise. It's something that's reliable like a trust mark. Even as an online business owner, you need to own a position in the minds of your current customers and prospective ones.

What do you wish to be known for in terms of (1) your expertise and (2) the type of business you run?

What are your core values? Think of three words that define your core values. When you face the question "What kind of business do you want to run?" think about what aligns with your core values.

1	2	3

What about **who you are, what you do, or why you do it** stands out to you?

What makes you, or your services unique?

Do you have a special process or approach? Do you do things differently from others or do you have a unique point of view than others do? If this question is challenging, identify ONE thing you believe sets you apart from others in your industry. What are you exceptionally good at?

How do you want customers to talk and feel about your brand?

What do your existing audience or customers say about your brand?
If you already have an audience, look out for cues as to what they're saying. What do they say in their emails to you? What do they say in their comments?

What about your brand do your clients/existing customers **rave** about?

Does what you think of your brand align with what your audience or ideal buyer thinks it is?

CREATE An Intensive Biz Playbook & Planner For Solopreneurs

Are your ideal customers able to identify you **as an expert in the 1–2 main** topics that you regularly share about? YES NO

What changes do you need to make to your content so that your ideal customers can easily connect you as an authority/expert in that area?

What business vices or bad habits do you have?

You may be thinking: *There are business vices?*

There sure are! Here are some examples: Buying new courses or new plugins. Jumping from creating one e-book to another without finishing the existing one. Reading income reports and mindless surfing. Knowing what these vices are will help you overcome them.

Note: But how do you know it's a vice? If you can go without it for 4–6 weeks comfortably without flinching or craving it, you don't have a bad habit. But if you're struggling to cut it out, that's a bad habit right there!

Vice	What will you do to help you cut this out of your day?
Surfing the web	Install an app to track hours spent surfing. Cut it down to 2 hours a week from 4.

What business-based fears are holding you back?

On his blog and in his TED talk, author Tim Ferriss talks about the importance of defining your fears rather than goals.[5] He terms it "fear setting" and says that it's the most important exercise to do if you want to conquer your fears. Once you define your fears, rate them on a scale of 1–10 with 10 being the worst. Ask yourself what's the worst that could happen if that fear plays out. How scared are you of each fear?

Fear	Rating from 1–10	Worst that can happen

What three skills would you like to learn in the next year? E.g., Facebook ads, graphic design, email marketing.

Skill	Who will you reach out to for help? E.g., a mentor, mastermind, or accountability buddy	What courses or programs will you take (if any)?	What resources will you access? E.g., specific podcasts or blogs that help with it

What three fears would you like to overcome in the next year? E.g., public speaking, Facebook Live, webinars.

Fear	Who will you reach out to for help? E.g., a mentor, mastermind, or accountability buddy	What courses or programs will you take (if any)?	What resources will you access? E.g., specific podcasts or blogs that help with it

What business tasks do you want to outsource next year? E.g., Pinterest management, graphic design.

Task	Who will you reach out to for help? E.g., a mentor, mastermind, or accountability buddy	What courses or programs will you take (if any)?	What resources will you access? E.g., specific podcasts or blogs that help with it

What business tools or tasks do you need to invest in or do for your brand to deliver on the vision you set out in the previous section? E.g., investing in a dedicated membership site, filing trademarks, investing in a sales page tool.

Business task/ tools	Date	Who will you approach or contact (if any)?	Comments	In progress	Completed
				○	○
				○	○
				○	○
				○	○
				○	○
				○	○
				○	○
				○	○
				○	○
				○	○
				○	○
				○	○
				○	○
				○	○
				○	○

YOUR CREATE SPACE

YOUR
MARKETING
MIX

"

Content builds relationships.
Relationships are built on trust.
Trust drives revenue

ANDREW DAVIS

Author & keynote speaker

Ever heard of the feast or famine cycle?

You have a high-income month where you've run a pretty successful product launch, or you have a calendar full of clients and make $6,000. But two months later, you're barely making $2,000 and wonder how you're going to pay your living and business expenses. Your revenue is never stable and is in a constant state of high and low. Sound familiar? Have you relegated it as an unavoidable aspect of business?

Many businesses do have high and low seasons. This could be because different times of the year affect your ideal customers. For instance, my client Rita runs a coaching program for stay-at-home moms, and summer is when she sees huge dips in traffic and revenue because most of her ideal customers have kids home from school. So how do you get out of this revenue yo-yo?

Is it really a case of high and low season or is there a deeper issue going on with how you handle your marketing that's affecting your revenue?

The feast or famine cycle is "the repeated pattern that service businesses get stuck in wherein they work diligently to secure new business, then having won that new business they have to stop doing their sales and marketing activities to fulfill on that work they just secured. But then they near completion of that work, they start to panic. 'We don't have any work in our funnel to replace that work with, and we've got overhead to cover and bills to pay." [6]

Is there a deeper issue going on with how you handle your marketing that's affecting your revenue?

The same goes for digital product creators. The months you launch are your best months, but you also know that your list can get tired and you can't possibly keep launching to the same group of people unless you add more people into your pipeline. Likewise, you may end up so tied up in the creation of a digital product that you completely neglect marketing activities that bring you customers in the first place. Those months where you're busy working on creation or development work, your revenue suffers.

When you neglect your marketing, you're not paying heed to the customer journey—specifically to the five types of people who come into contact with your business and brand.

1. Strangers

They haven't heard of you before at all. They probably clicked onto your site from seeing a pin image on Pinterest, a Facebook post that a friend of theirs shared, or a tweet on their Twitter feed. Should you try to capture all of these readers?

No, because not all of them will be your ideal reader. But you need to make sure you're continuously putting your business in front of new audiences so that they have the opportunity to find your business. There are plenty of ways you can do this—e.g., paying for ads, podcasts, guest posts, guest speaking, summits, etc. Most of these do involve pitching another party.

2. Readers

They have some form of brand recognition. They've heard of you before via a podcast or seen you guest post on a site they frequent. A friend of theirs has been raving about you. They've clicked through to your site to read your content.

3. Subscribers

They are new to your list. They visit your site likely from a link in your welcome email series. They may have read something intriguing in your sequence of emails and wanted to have a look at your blog, YouTube channel, or other content platforms.

4. Engaged subscribers

Heard of a brand crush? That's what these people have with you. They adore your style. Most of them cannot wait to get their hands on your paid products if they haven't already. They look to your brand to help them and see you as trustworthy.

5. Customers & Brand advocates

These are people who are attuned to your style. They've likely bought from you before—possibly more than once. They also spread the word out about your brand without you even asking them to do it.

Each of these different segments offers a unique opportunity for your business. And you need all of these different segments in your business. Your business needs to make an effort to

1. Get more people on the front end. This is how you continuously fill your sales pipeline with "leads" or potential customers.
2. Constantly nudge people from one segment to the next. The further down the sales pipeline people are, the better it is for your business.

When both these processes stop, you have a situation where your email list can go stale and contacts can go cold because there's no process in place for others to discover your business or to nurture new subscribers.

In this section, you'll explore **a.** how you can make your marketing efforts "evergreen" so that you can use them again and again and **b.** how you can automate more of your marketing so that you have less on your plate.

What marketing activities are currently working for your business?

Marketing activities are any activities that help you move potential customers through the four-step process (Attract – Capture – Engage – Convert) that I introduced at the start of the workbook. Where did your current and past customers come from? Review traffic sources and activities that have helped your customers find you.

Marketing Activity	Keep	Cull or do less of	Comments
Pinterest marketing	○	○	Increase the no. of pins created per content piece
	○	○	
	○	○	
	○	○	
	○	○	
	○	○	
	○	○	
	○	○	
	○	○	

Is there an overreliance on any particular marketing activity? What can you do to curb this?

What marketing activities do you enjoy?

Focus on activities that you are willing to commit to and that you'll be motivated to spend enough time on to get results. Add on any that you think fit into the table.

	You thrive here	Like	Dislike
Attending events (Trade shows or conferences)		○	○
Public speaking		○	○
Writing or creating training materials or info products		○	○
Writing copy (e.g., emails, sales pages, blog posts)		○	○
Creating videos		○	○
Recording audios		○	○
Networking live (in person)		○	○
Networking online in forums and groups		○	○
Podcasts		○	○
Guest posting		○	○
Creating visuals or graphics		○	○
Self-publishing		○	○
Live workshops/ webinars		○	○
Ads		○	○
		○	○
		○	○
		○	○
		○	○
		○	○
		○	○

Which of these marketing activities can you automate, but haven't yet? E.g., start compiling common FAQs in one place where you can refer people to. Create templates for your graphics. Have a nurture sequence go out on auto to new subscribers.

If you couldn't fail, what marketing activities would you like to try? E.g., offer a pay-what you-want pricing model, run a challenge or summer school, host an in-person event, etc.

Activity	Who will you reach out to for help? E.g., a mentor, mastermind, or accountability buddy	What resources will you access? E.g., specific podcasts or blogs help with it	When can you execute it?

What will you do to get more of each type of segment not only discovering your business but exploring and realizing the full potential and possibilities of working with you?

	What will you do to get more of this segment?	What are you doing to move them a step forward?	Where do you struggle the most with this segment?	List one single intention you have for this segment
Stranger				
Readers				
Subscribers				
Engaged Subscribers				
Brand Advocates *What will you do to retain brand advocates?				

CREATE An Intensive Biz Playbook & Planner For Solopreneurs

Where are there drop-off points or missed opportunities for each segment?

E.g., you don't have a nurture sequence after someone signs up to your email list. You don't segment your subscribers. You are not consistent with your email marketing with regard to tone and frequency.

	Missed Opportunities
Stranger	
Readers	
Subscribers	
Engaged Subscribers	
Brand Advocates *What will you do to retain brand advocates?*	

What part of this process can you put into systems, but haven't yet?

How will you get your business in front of new audiences next year?
List all contact points you will reach out to.

Contact	Ideas	Pitched/Contacted	Booked	Not Successful	Follow-up	Comments
		○	○	○	○	
		○	○	○	○	
		○	○	○	○	
		○	○	○	○	
		○	○	○	○	
		○	○	○	○	
		○	○	○	○	
		○	○	○	○	
		○	○	○	○	
		○	○	○	○	
		○	○	○	○	
		○	○	○	○	

Do you offer existing clients or customers a way to continue working with you after a project or course? What would make it easy for them to do so and what can you offer? What opportunities are you potentially overlooking? How can you be a continuous partner who is vested in their success—e.g., brainstorm or strategy session, monthly trainings or check-ins, resource curations, etc.

CAPTURING YOUR AUDIENCE WITH LEAD MAGNETS

Does your lead magnet still work? What may have been a novel lead magnet a year or two ago may not be anymore because more of your competitors have started to use it too. Is it fair? Sure, it isn't. And if yours is still doing a better job than the rest of your competitors, go ahead and keep it. Or better, work on refreshing it.

How can you refresh an opt-in?

- Increase the content. If you're offering a lead magnet pegged to a number (e.g., 20 templates or 100 cold email scripts), increase the number.
- Upgrade the design (cover, inner pages, title). Add bullet points on your opt-in forms to make them more attractive.
- Can you try a different capture method? E.g., switch your exit intent pop-up to a top bar or scroll box?

But lead magnets can grow stale as well. If your conversions are dwindling no matter how much you promote and optimize your forms and landing pages, it's time to try something different. If so, I'd suggest killing your lead magnet. No matter what new lead magnet you create, make sure that it's aligned with your business, and it leads to specific paid offers or future offers that you may develop.

Name of primary lead magnet(s)	Results	Still aligned with business?	Keep	Refresh	Kill	Comments
			○	○	○	
			○	○	○	
			○	○	○	
			○	○	○	
			○	○	○	
			○	○	○	

*Primary lead magnets are the ones responsible for the majority of your subscribers

What new ideas do you have for lead magnets or opt-in freebies? For each lead magnet idea, make sure it flows into your business and/or your offers.

New lead magnet	Date of release	Comments	Outline	Draft	Edit	Publish
			○	○	○	○
			○	○	○	○
			○	○	○	○
			○	○	○	○
			○	○	○	○
			○	○	○	○

YOUR CREATE SPACE

YOUR
DIGITAL
PRESENCE

"

Entrepreneurship is neither
a science nor an art.
It is a practice.

PETER DRUCKER

Management consultant, educator, and author

I knew people were getting mixed signals about what I was doing when I read these two comments on two completely different sites.

But Meera has moved into content marketing now…

Meera is known for digital products.

My first thought: *Whatever gave them that idea?*

My specialty is email marketing. Yes, I do have a book on content planning. Yes, I do have a course on product creation. But both always circle back to the importance of email. Somewhere along the way, the message about who I served and what I helped people with got lost.

When people start getting mixed signals about what you do, it's time for you to pause and reflect. There are two things that could be wrong here:

1. Your digital presence—which includes your entire site as well as your social media profiles—is communicating the wrong message about what you're doing or is not communicating any message at all.

2. The way you're projecting your brand is not aligned with how you want it to be perceived. We discussed this in the section Your Zone of Genius.

> When people start getting mixed signals about what you do, it's time for you to pause and reflect

Can it be fixed? It sure can. But it depends on whether the issue is twofold. Most issues with your digital presence are cosmetic and can be corrected quickly if you know exactly what and who you want to help. But an issue with your brand message could take longer to fix.

Let's talk about your digital presence first. Your digital presence, like your brand, has a shelf life. It ages. Depending on the industry you serve, things may move faster, and you may find yourself needing to take a closer look at how your digital presence communicates your message.

In this section, let's focus on your site. And no, I'm not referring to your home page. Your home page is important, but I do think we put too much emphasis and pressure on getting the home page right at the expense of other areas of our site. Most visitors are likely to click through to other pages on your site—not your home page. Have a look at your Google Analytics, and you'll find that to be true.

What's the primary goal of your site? E.g., to capture readers and turn them into subscribers? To get them to trial your service? To get them to check out your store?

Does your website pass the five-second test?[7] Studies have found that visitors only spend a few seconds assessing your website before deciding whether to stay or leave.[8] Within the first 5–10 seconds, will your ideal customer be able to tell what you do and why they should choose you? And why do you think so?

If you suspect that your website would probably fail the five-second test, then here's where you craft a one-liner or "What do you do" statement for your brand. The perfect one-liner is

◯ What your ideal customers wants ◯ Short enough to fit into one sentence

◯ Clear and specific

In *StoryBrand*,[9] Donald Miller suggests creating a four-part one-liner statement. The statement would include (1) the character (who you are helping), (2) the problem (that you're helping to solve), (3) the plan (how are you going to help them), and (4) the success (what's the outcome).

Another way of looking at it is simply: What you do – Who you help – Your benefit

State your one-liner here:

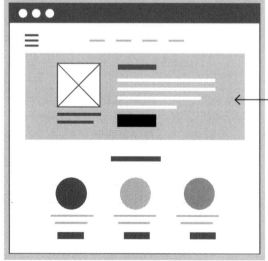

Note: A prime spot for the one-liner on your website is the header (see image below). This is where a one-liner or "What do you do" statement will fit in because it's immediately visible.

What changes do you need to make to your site so that your ideal customers can easily connect you as an authority/expert in your area of expertise?

Does your site align with your brand visually? Does your site give off the same vibe and tone that your brand does? ◯ YES ◯ NO

If not, what can you do?

Does it look current or dated? Fashion and tastes change, and you can visually spot a website designed in 2018 versus 2013. You don't want your site to say that your brand is stale. What changes can you make?

Based on your goal, does it drive your ideal customers to clear and logical next steps? If not, what changes do you need to make? E.g., if your goal is to capture readers and convert them to subscribers, is your opt-in the main focus on your site?

What is sorely missing on your site? Think about the four components of the marketing system (Attract – Capture – Engage – Convert). What pieces do you need to add to your site to enhance and boost each of these components? E.g., a shop page? An about page? Testimonials?

Attract	→	Capture	→	Engage	→	Convert

One of the main building blocks you need to pay attention to is your navigation bar. Write in your current navigation bar categories (draw in your drop-downs).

....
....
....
....
....
....
....
....

For each navigation page or category, consider the following:

○ Is this page something your reader has to absolutely see or visit?
○ Is this page crucial to brand awareness, to build trust, or to make sales?
○ If there are drop-downs, are the drop-downs necessary? Can you add that page elsewhere?

With these considerations, craft your new navigation.

New navigation

....
....
....
....
....
....
....
....

What do you have but need to refresh?

If it needs to be refreshed, plot in your deadline as well as stage of progress as you work on it.

	Keep	Refresh	Outline	Draft	Edit	Complete	Comments
Privacy policy							
Headshots							
Header images							
Shop page (to include new products)							
About page							
Contact form							
GDPR compliance							
Email signature							
Social share icons							
Logo							
Social media templates							

What other information do readers or subscribers always ask you about that needs to be included on your webpage? Where can you include this information? E.g., how to sign up to be an affiliate? What products do you have? Do you accept guest posts? Location or map if you also have a physical store?

For each piece of information, where do these queries usually reach you from? From your email list? From your contact form? These will give you important clues about where you can include the information.

List three small things that you can do that will make the biggest impact on your website.

1. ....

....

2. ....

....

3. ....

....

YOUR OFFERS (PRODUCTS & SERVICES)

"

Don't wait for perfection. Life isn't perfect. Do the best you can and ship. Real people ship, and then they test and then they ship again.
Then you wake up one day and you have something insanely great."

GUY KAWASAKI

Entrepreneur

I had a reader who couldn't commit to her existing offers.

When I asked about when she'd be relaunching one of her offers, she'd say: *I'm not sure if I'm going to offer it again.*

Then she would ax the product, announce it to her list, and move on to the next one.

I couldn't quite understand why. I knew she was frustrated with her sales (or lack thereof).

But is that reason enough to kill a product? Especially if you've only launched it once?

It's unlikely that your product is the culprit (especially if you've done some degree of due diligence before creating it). It could simply be that you need to repackage your offer and position it differently.

Your offer is a marketing asset. A good marketing asset is one that you can sell year after year. Of course, I'm not suggesting keeping it the way it is. Just like your home is an asset that needs maintenance, repair, and a fresh coat of paint, your offer needs to be updated, tweaked, and repackaged.

In this case, one of the reasons for the lack of sales could be that the offer's messaging needs to be tweaked so that it resonates with her audience. A messaging that worked once may not work again.

Why?

Because your audience may have shifted...

Your niche may have shifted...

But what if you already have something that works?

Should you mess with something that's working?

Don't think of it as messing but staying current with the market. Because remember that the

> It's unlikely that your product is the culprit. It could simply be that you need to repackage your offer and position it differently

market shifts. Key messages change. When I started blogging about email marketing a few years ago, the key message in the niche was "an email list is important—so start one." Now though, almost everyone understands that an email list is important, so the awareness level of the audience and the social conversation surrounding the topic has shifted. These are things you need to look out for and reframe so that your product message stays fresh.

YOUR IDEAL BUYER – WHO ARE THEY?

You'll get different types of buyers for each of your offers—buyers who are at different ends of the spectrum. You can identify them from the five states of awareness, which is something I mention in my book *Your First 100* as well as in the *CREATE* planner.

A visitor is likely to be **Problem Unaware** if they haven't yet identified their pain or problem
A visitor is likely to be **Problem Aware** if they are aware of what they need help with
A visitor is likely to be **Solution Unaware** when they've felt pain but have not discovered that solutions exist for it (have not started "shopping" around)
A visitor is likely to be **Solution Aware** when they know that a problem exists and they have discovered that solutions exist for it (they have started "shopping" around)
Most Aware of problem that needs to be solved and how your offer helps them solve it

While you can have content at each of these junctures, your offer should only speak to one person. You don't sell your products to everybody. Of course, you're free to do so.

But you don't actively try to attract everyone. You only need to spend your time and resources attracting your ideal customer. Keep these people at the center and focus your efforts here so you attract more of them.

When your ideal reader is problem unaware, start by introducing them to the problem that others similar to them have. When your ideal reader is problem aware, start the discussion by talking about the issue at hand. Get them to identify with it and acknowledge the difficulties they are having. When your ideal reader is solution aware, start by giving them a unique insight into the "solution" landscape.

In my program Email Lists Simplified, my ideal customer is someone who is problem aware. They understand the importance of email but don't know how the pieces fit together. I'm not targeting the skeptics (people skeptical that email marketing will work) because they are not my ideal customers.

In my program Product in 7, my ideal customer is solution aware. I start the discussion and engage my ideal customer by talking about existing solutions out there and position mine as the unique alternative.

So you'll pitch your offers differently to different types of buyers.

INCHING YOUR IDEAL BUYER TO 'YES'

Now that you know how to position your offer and who exactly your ideal buyer is, let's discuss what will inch your ideal buyer to saying yes to your offer.

1. Do they buy into your USP (unique selling proposition) or positioning statement?

What big benefit will they buy into?

What benefit does your ideal reader want that others are not promising?

What does your product do that nobody else's does?

Why should they buy from you instead of anybody else?

What guarantee can you make that nobody else can make?

Your USP or positioning statement is the answer to these questions. As a marketer you need to know the answers to these questions to constantly improve the use of whatever you sell.

E.g., Email Lists Simplified (ELS) is an A–Z email marketing course for solopreneurs and small business owners who need help with all aspects of email marketing. Unlike other courses that focus solely on list building or one single aspect of email marketing, ELS takes a holistic approach to email marketing and covers strategy, email editorial calendars, re-engagement, and writing sequences so that you will know how to create an email marketing strategy for your business.

E.g., Product in 7 (Pi7) is a templatized product creation process for solopreneurs and small business owners who are overwhelmed with the thought of creating their first or next digital product. Unlike other programs that teach product creation, Pi7 focuses on baking marketing into the product creation so that you are guaranteed to make sales.

2. Do they have the ability to say YES and does it fit their overall plans?

If your ideal buyer is interested but is not able to say YES to your offer, you've still lost the sale.

E.g., if your ideal reader is a stay-at-home mom and your offer is a retreat conducted in July, many of them are not going to be able to attend especially if they have school-going kids who are home for the summer.

3. Are you helping your ideal buyer overcome buyer resistance?

Every ideal buyer will have their own set of ifs and buts. These false beliefs and assumptions will stop your reader from taking action. It keeps them in their current state acting as a form of resistance. Knowing what those ifs and buts are will help you create content that helps them overcome their doubts.

- I don't have a choice; I have to…
- I can only achieve X if I get Y
- It will not work for me
- It's too late
- There's a secret people are keeping from me
- This has to be difficult
- I'm not worthy
- Why would they listen to me

- I'm a fraud
- There's only so much
- More is better
- I'll do it after I get X
- You need six figures to…
- I can't trust anyone
- I've tried and failed. This time won't be any different
- It's always been hard for me

4. People look to justify their emotional buying with logic. Are you helping them do it?

Once sold, people need to satisfy their buying decision with logic. So don't ask "What don't you like about the program?" in your welcome or feedback email. That's actually going to make them feel worse about their decision. What are you doing to help them justify their purchase? Do you have a support group? An onboarding sequence? Are you re-emphasizing the guarantee to take away their anxiety?

In this section, you're going to uncover a series of questions that will help you polish your existing offers. Rather than discarding your offer and moving on to create something new, if you take stock of the messaging behind the product and how it compares to other products out there, you'll be able to breathe life into an offer that you think is going stale.

There is space to do this exercise for five of your existing offers.

If you need more, I have a set of free printables you can download from **CREATEPLANNER. COM/WORKBOOK-BONUS.**

OFFER 1

Name of offer: ....

My ideal buyer is... but..

Problem unaware/
Problem aware/solution unaware/
solution aware

Main pain
point/bleeding
neck

I'm not actively targeting ....

Who are not your target audience?

State your product positioning statement (use the prompts above):

How much did this offer make you last year?

If you are selling this on a few different storefronts and have the data, list how much each platform made? Or if you have buyers coming in from a few different entry points, sketch this out in the pie chart.

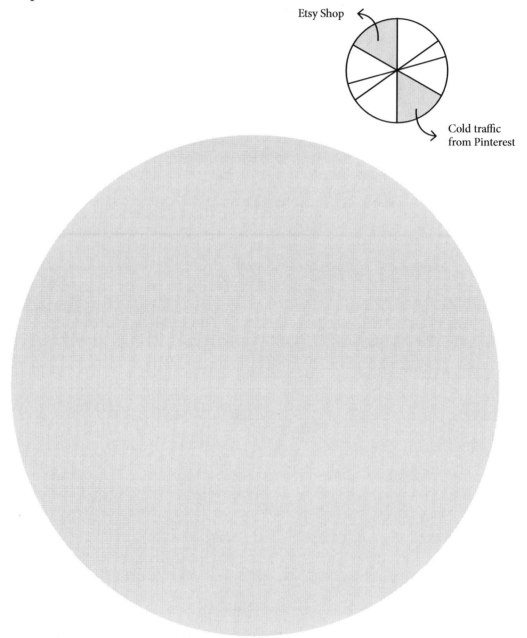

Etsy Shop

Cold traffic from Pinterest

What could have been done better to improve sales on each platform?

Platform	What worked?	What didn't?	What could have been done better?

What marketing assets do you have for this offer?

Type	Goal	Keep	Refresh	Kill	Comments
Email challenge	Segment email list for launch	○	○	○	Start promotions earlier. Add a live video component to the challenge.
		○	○	○	
		○	○	○	
		○	○	○	
		○	○	○	
		○	○	○	
		○	○	○	

Analyze the offer against the underlying drivers discussed in this section of the book.

○ Does your ideal buyer they have the ability to say YES and does it fit their overall plans?

○ Does your ideal buyer buy into your USP or positioning statement?

○ Are you helping your ideal buyer overcome buyer resistance? E.g., through prelaunch content, email sequences, etc.

○ Your ideal buyer will look to justify their emotional buying with logic. Are you helping them to justify it?

Do a competitor analysis for competing products of this offer.

Product Name	Headline or Promise	Bonuses Offered	Loopholes/ Gaps in Offer	Price Point

Based on your responses above, what needs to be changed or reframed in your offer?

Are there any elements that may be creating confusion? E.g., dig into questions raised most often by prospective buyers. What questions do they ask?

Do you have multiple tiers that may be causing buyer indecisiveness?

How much do you want to earn from this offer next year? Use how much this offer earned this year to project sales.

Where are you missing out on opportunities? Think in terms of the marketing system diagram below and what you can do to meet or exceed your goals—e.g., you don't have sufficient entry points for a subscriber to experience your sales funnel for this offer. You don't have a nurture sequence for lead magnets that lead into this offer.

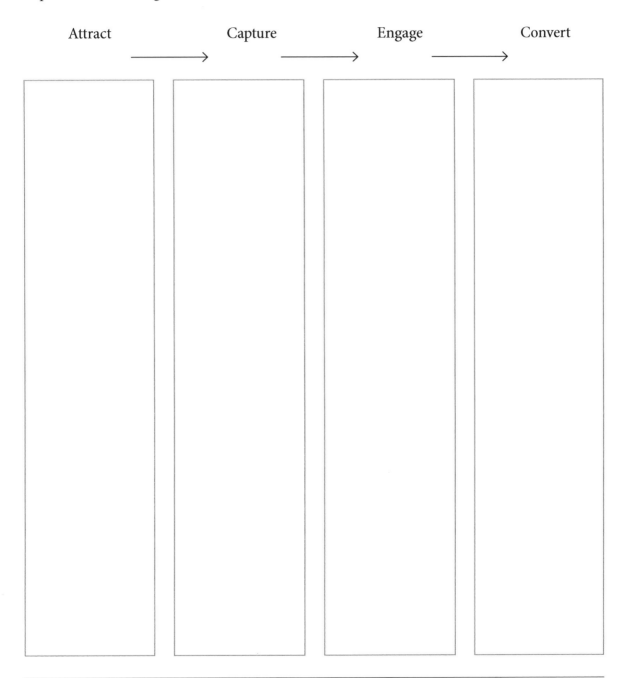

Attract   Capture   Engage   Convert

Based on how much you want this offer to earn next year, answer the following questions:

a. When and how many times do you plan to launch or hold campaigns for this offer? Include sales promotions as well as active launches.

b. If your goal is to make 20K from this offer and you plan to hold two active launches and two under-the-radar or email-only launches, what are your estimated sales for each launch?

c. How many sign-ups or opt-ins do you need to meet this goal?

Dig into your previous data. For example, let's say you had 1,000 people sign up for a challenge and had a 4% conversion rate (40 sales) for the price of your offer. If your goal for next year is to increase the sales numbers to 60, you need to get 1,500 sign-ups for the challenge. If your conversion rate is 2%, but you still want 40 sales, you need to get 1,800 sign-ups. Fill in the data for each potential launch. This helps you see what you're working toward.

Launch Dates/ Campaigns	Goal/ Estimated Sales	Marketing Assets	Past Performance	No. of Opt-ins Needed
15 May 20XX	60 sales at $397	Challenge Quiz	40 sales for 1,000 sign-ups. 4% conversion rate	1,500

*Skip Launch Dates section if your offer is evergreen.

CREATE An Intensive Biz Playbook & Planner For Solopreneurs

What additional marketing assets would you like to create? Leave this blank if you need to.

List three quick things (just three) that you can do that will make the biggest impact on this offer—or will really move the needle with your results. These can be additions or improvements to the existing offer in any of the four components of the marketing process (Attract – Capture – Engage – Convert).

1. ....
....

2. ....
....

3. ....
....

OFFER 2

Name of offer: ....

My ideal buyer is... but...

Problem unaware/
Problem aware/solution unaware
/solution aware

Main pain
point/bleeding
neck

I'm not actively targeting ....

Who are not your target audience?

State your product positioning statement (use the prompts above):

How much did this offer make you last year?

If you are selling this on a few different storefronts and have the data, list how much each platform made? Or if you have buyers coming in from a few different entry points, sketch this out in the pie chart.

What could have been done better to improve sales on each platform?

Platform	What worked?	What didn't?	What could have been done better?

CREATE An Intensive Biz Playbook & Planner For Solopreneurs

What marketing assets do you have for this offer?

Type	Goal	Keep	Refresh	Kill	Comments
		○	○	○	
		○	○	○	
		○	○	○	
		○	○	○	
		○	○	○	
		○	○	○	
		○	○	○	

Analyze the offer against the underlying drivers discussed in this section of the book.

○ Does your ideal buyer they have the ability to say YES and does it fit their overall plans?

○ Does your ideal buyer buy into your USP or positioning statement?

○ Are you helping your ideal buyer overcome buyer resistance? E.g., through prelaunch content, email sequences, etc.

○ Your ideal buyer will look to justify their emotional buying with logic. Are you helping them to justify it?

Do a competitor analysis for competing products of this offer.

Product Name	Headline or Promise	Bonuses Offered	Loopholes/ Gaps in Offer	Price Point

Based on your responses above, what needs to be changed or reframed in your offer?

Are there any elements that may be creating confusion? E.g., dig into questions raised most often by prospective buyers. What questions do they ask?

Do you have multiple tiers that may be causing buyer indecisiveness?

How much do you want to earn from this offer next year? Use how much this offer earned this year to project sales.

Where are you missing out on opportunities? Think in terms of the marketing system diagram below and what you can do to meet or exceed your goals—e.g., you don't have sufficient entry points for a subscriber to experience your sales funnel for this offer. You don't have a nurture sequence for lead magnets that lead into this offer.

Attract	→	Capture	→	Engage	→	Convert

CREATE An Intensive Biz Playbook & Planner For Solopreneurs

Based on how much you want this offer to earn next year, answer the following questions:

a. When and how many times do you plan to launch or hold campaigns for this offer? Include sales promotions as well as active launches.

b. If your goal is to make 20K from this offer and you plan to hold two active launches and two under-the-radar or email-only launches, what are your estimated sales for each launch?

c. How many sign-ups or opt-ins do you need to meet this goal?

Dig into your previous data. For example, let's say you had 1,000 people sign up for a challenge and had a 4% conversion rate (40 sales) for the price of your offer. If your goal for next year is to increase the sales numbers to 60, you need to get 1,500 sign-ups for the challenge. If your conversion rate is 2%, but you still want 40 sales, you need to get 1,800 sign-ups. Fill in the data for each potential launch. This helps you see what you're working toward.

Launch Dates/ Campaigns	Goal/ Estimated Sales	Marketing Assets	Past Performance	No. of Opt-ins Needed

*Skip Launch Dates section if your offer is evergreen.

What additional marketing assets would you like to create? Leave this blank if you need to.

List three quick things (just three) that you can do that will make the biggest impact on this offer—or will really move the needle with your results. These can be additions or improvements to the existing offer in any of the four components of the marketing process (Attract – Capture – Engage – Convert).

1. ....

....

2. ....

....

3. ....

....

YOUR CREATE SPACE

OFFER 3

Name of offer: ....

My ideal buyer is... but...

Problem unaware/
Problem aware/solution unaware
/solution aware

Main pain
point/bleeding
neck

I'm not actively targeting ....

Who are not your target audience?

State your product positioning statement (use the prompts above):

How much did this offer make you last year?

If you are selling this on a few different storefronts and have the data, list how much each platform made? Or if you have buyers coming in from a few different entry points, sketch this out in the pie chart.

What could have been done better to improve sales on each platform?

Platform	What worked?	What didn't?	What could have been done better?

CREATE An Intensive Biz Playbook & Planner For Solopreneurs

What marketing assets do you have for this offer?

Type	Goal	Keep	Refresh	Kill	Comments
		○	○	○	
		○	○	○	
		○	○	○	
		○	○	○	
		○	○	○	
		○	○	○	
		○	○	○	

Analyze the offer against the underlying drivers discussed in this section of the book.

○   Does your ideal buyer they have the ability to say YES and does it fit their overall plans?

○   Does your ideal buyer buy into your USP or positioning statement?

○   Are you helping your ideal buyer overcome buyer resistance? E.g., through prelaunch content, email sequences, etc.

○   Your ideal buyer will look to justify their emotional buying with logic. Are you helping them to justify it?

Do a competitor analysis for competing products of this offer.

Product Name	Headline or Promise	Bonuses Offered	Loopholes/ Gaps in Offer	Price Point

Based on your responses above, what needs to be changed or reframed in your offer?

CREATE An Intensive Biz Playbook & Planner For Solopreneurs

Are there any elements that may be creating confusion? E.g., dig into questions raised most often by prospective buyers. What questions do they ask?

Do you have multiple tiers that may be causing buyer indecisiveness?

How much do you want to earn from this offer next year? Use how much this offer earned this year to project sales.

Where are you missing out on opportunities? Think in terms of the marketing system diagram below and what you can do to meet or exceed your goals—e.g., you don't have sufficient entry points for a subscriber to experience your sales funnel for this offer. You don't have a nurture sequence for lead magnets that lead into this offer.

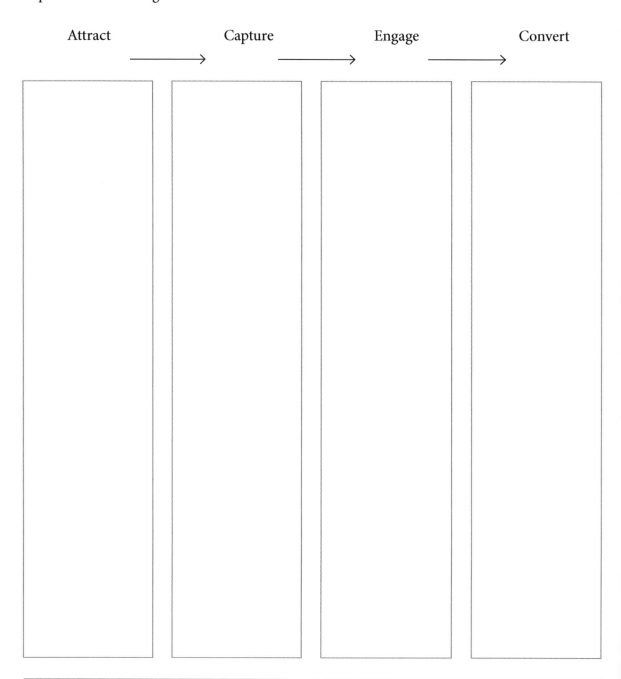

Attract	Capture	Engage	Convert

Based on how much you want this offer to earn next year, answer the following questions:

a. When and how many times do you plan to launch or hold campaigns for this offer? Include sales promotions as well as active launches.

b. If your goal is to make 20K from this offer and you plan to hold two active launches and two under-the-radar or email-only launches, what are your estimated sales for each launch?

c. How many sign-ups or opt-ins do you need to meet this goal?

Dig into your previous data. For example, let's say you had 1,000 people sign up for a challenge and had a 4% conversion rate (40 sales) for the price of your offer. If your goal for next year is to increase the sales numbers to 60, you need to get 1,500 sign-ups for the challenge. If your conversion rate is 2%, but you still want 40 sales, you need to get 1,800 sign-ups. Fill in the data for each potential launch. This helps you see what you're working toward.

Launch Dates/ Campaigns	Goal/ Estimated Sales	Marketing Assets	Past Performance	No. of Opt-ins Needed

*Skip Launch Dates section if your offer is evergreen.

What additional marketing assets would you like to create? Leave this blank if you need to.

List three quick things (just three) that you can do that will make the biggest impact on this offer—or will really move the needle with your results. These can be additions or improvements to the existing offer in any of the four components of the marketing process (Attract – Capture – Engage – Convert).

1. ....

....

2. ....

....

3. ....

....

YOUR CREATE SPACE

OFFER 4

Name of offer: ....

My ideal buyer is.. but...

Problem unaware/
Problem aware/solution unaware
/solution aware

Main pain
point/bleeding
neck

I'm not actively targeting ....

Who are not your target audience?

State your product positioning statement (use the prompts above):

How much did this offer make you last year?

If you are selling this on a few different storefronts and have the data, list how much each platform made? Or if you have buyers coming in from a few different entry points, sketch this out in the pie chart.

What could have been done better to improve sales on each platform?

Platform	What worked?	What didn't?	What could have been done better?

CREATE An Intensive Biz Playbook & Planner For Solopreneurs

What marketing assets do you have for this offer?

Type	Goal	Keep	Refresh	Kill	Comments
		○	○	○	
		○	○	○	
		○	○	○	
		○	○	○	
		○	○	○	
		○	○	○	
		○	○	○	

Analyze the offer against the underlying drivers discussed in this section of the book.

○ Does your ideal buyer they have the ability to say YES and does it fit their overall plans?

○ Does your ideal buyer buy into your USP or positioning statement?

○ Are you helping your ideal buyer overcome buyer resistance? E.g., through prelaunch content, email sequences, etc.

○ Your ideal buyer will look to justify their emotional buying with logic. Are you helping them to justify it?

Do a competitor analysis for competing products of this offer.

Product Name	Headline or Promise	Bonuses Offered	Loopholes/ Gaps in Offer	Price Point

Based on your responses above, what needs to be changed or reframed in your offer?

Are there any elements that may be creating confusion? E.g., dig into questions raised most often by prospective buyers. What questions do they ask?

Do you have multiple tiers that may be causing buyer indecisiveness?

How much do you want to earn from this offer next year? Use how much this offer earned this year to project sales.

Where are you missing out on opportunities? Think in terms of the marketing system diagram below and what you can do to meet or exceed your goals—e.g., you don't have sufficient entry points for a subscriber to experience your sales funnel for this offer. You don't have a nurture sequence for lead magnets that lead into this offer.

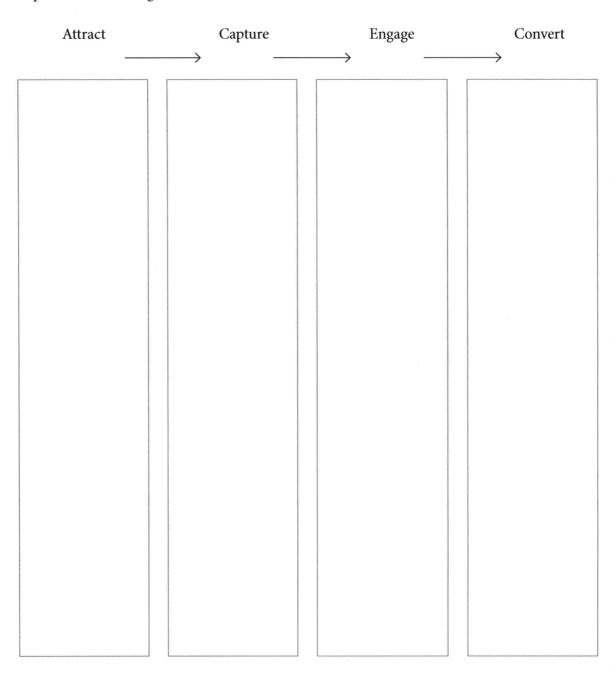

Attract	Capture	Engage	Convert

Based on how much you want this offer to earn next year, answer the following questions:

a. When and how many times do you plan to launch or hold campaigns for this offer? Include sales promotions as well as active launches.

b. If your goal is to make 20K from this offer and you plan to hold two active launches and two under-the-radar or email-only launches, what are your estimated sales for each launch?

c. How many sign-ups or opt-ins do you need to meet this goal?

Dig into your previous data. For example, let's say you had 1,000 people sign up for a challenge and had a 4% conversion rate (40 sales) for the price of your offer. If your goal for next year is to increase the sales numbers to 60, you need to get 1,500 sign-ups for the challenge. If your conversion rate is 2%, but you still want 40 sales, you need to get 1,800 sign-ups. Fill in the data for each potential launch. This helps you see what you're working toward.

Launch Dates/ Campaigns	Goal/ Estimated Sales	Marketing Assets	Past Performance	No. of Opt-ins Needed

*Skip Launch Dates section if your offer is evergreen.

What additional marketing assets would you like to create? Leave this blank if you need to.

List three quick things (just three) that you can do that will make the biggest impact on this offer—or will really move the needle with your results. These can be additions or improvements to the existing offer in any of the four components of the marketing process (Attract – Capture – Engage – Convert).

1. ....

....

2. ....

....

3. ....

....

OFFER 5

Name of offer: ....

My ideal buyer is... but...

Problem unaware/
Problem aware/solution unaware
/solution aware

Main pain
point/bleeding
neck

I'm not actively targeting ....

Who are not your target audience?

State your product positioning statement (use the prompts above):

How much did this offer make you last year?

If you are selling this on a few different storefronts and have the data, list how much each platform made? Or if you have buyers coming in from a few different entry points, sketch this out in the pie chart.

What could have been done better to improve sales on each platform?

Platform	What worked?	What didn't?	What could have been done better?

What marketing assets do you have for this offer?

Type	Goal	Keep	Refresh	Kill	Comments
		○	○	○	
		○	○	○	
		○	○	○	
		○	○	○	
		○	○	○	
		○	○	○	
		○	○	○	

Analyze the offer against the underlying drivers discussed in this section of the book.

○ Does your ideal buyer they have the ability to say YES and does it fit their overall plans?

○ Does your ideal buyer buy into your USP or positioning statement?

○ Are you helping your ideal buyer overcome buyer resistance? E.g., through prelaunch content, email sequences, etc.

○ Your ideal buyer will look to justify their emotional buying with logic. Are you helping them to justify it?

Do a competitor analysis for competing products of this offer.

Product Name	Headline or Promise	Bonuses Offered	Loopholes/ Gaps in Offer	Price Point

Based on your responses above, what needs to be changed or reframed in your offer?

CREATE An Intensive Biz Playbook & Planner For Solopreneurs

Are there any elements that may be creating confusion? E.g., dig into questions raised most often by prospective buyers. What questions do they ask?

Do you have multiple tiers that may be causing buyer indecisiveness?

How much do you want to earn from this offer next year? Use how much this offer earned this year to project sales.

Where are you missing out on opportunities? Think in terms of the marketing system diagram below and what you can do to meet or exceed your goals—e.g., you don't have sufficient entry points for a subscriber to experience your sales funnel for this offer. You don't have a nurture sequence for lead magnets that lead into this offer.

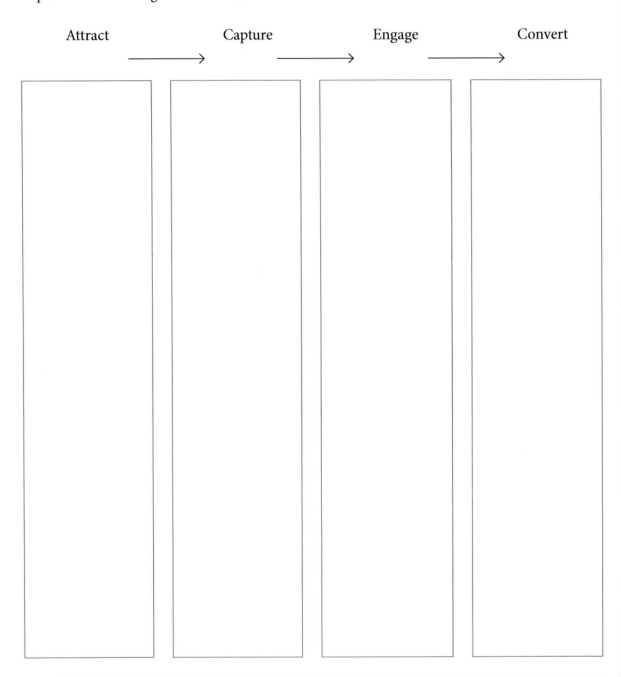

Attract　　　　　Capture　　　　　Engage　　　　　Convert

Based on how much you want this offer to earn next year, answer the following questions:

a. When and how many times do you plan to launch or hold campaigns for this offer? Include sales promotions as well as active launches.

b. If your goal is to make 20K from this offer and you plan to hold two active launches and two under-the-radar or email-only launches, what are your estimated sales for each launch?

c. How many sign-ups or opt-ins do you need to meet this goal?

Dig into your previous data. For example, let's say you had 1,000 people sign up for a challenge and had a 4% conversion rate (40 sales) for the price of your offer. If your goal for next year is to increase the sales numbers to 60, you need to get 1,500 sign-ups for the challenge. If your conversion rate is 2%, but you still want 40 sales, you need to get 1,800 sign-ups. Fill in the data for each potential launch. This helps you see what you're working toward.

Launch Dates/ Campaigns	Goal/ Estimated Sales	Marketing Assets	Past Performance	No. of Opt-ins Needed

*Skip Launch Dates section if your offer is evergreen.

What additional marketing assets would you like to create? Leave this blank if you need to.

List three quick things (just three) that you can do that will make the biggest impact on this offer—or will really move the needle with your results. These can be additions or improvements to the existing offer in any of the four components of the marketing process (Attract – Capture – Engage – Convert).

1. ....

....

2. ....

....

3. ....

....

YOUR CREATE SPACE

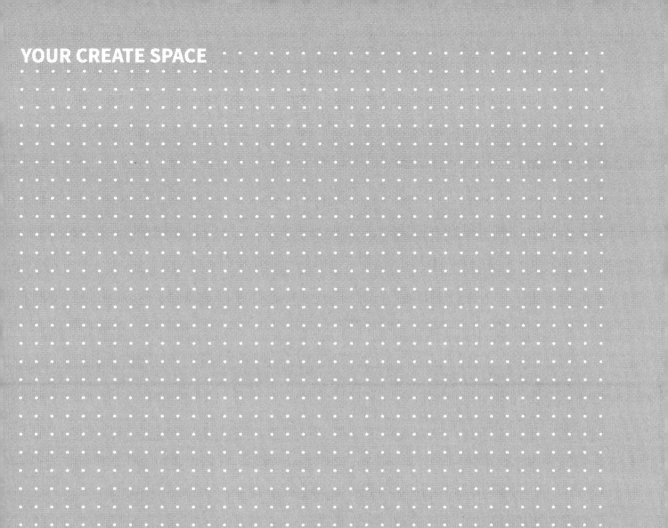

YOUR
REVENUE
& INCOME
PLAN

"

Don't settle: Don't finish crappy books. If you don't like the menu, leave the restaurant. If you're not on the right path, get off it."

CHRIS BROGAN

CEO of Owner Media Group

How many streams of revenue should you have?

In the book *Stop Hustling Gigs and Start Building a Business,*[10] author Joel Block mentions the term Revenue Octopus. He states that "in order to create or sustain hyper growth, a business has to have eight different revenue streams." You want to avoid an overreliance on any one revenue source, just like you want to avoid an overreliance on any one traffic source.

Note: Revenue is the total of what your business generates in terms of earnings.

There are three ways you can do this:

1. Add a completely **new** revenue source. This could include consulting, public speaking, affiliate marketing, joint ventures, or digital products.

2. Go **wider** on an existing revenue source—e.g., repurposing a product into a different marketplace to reach a new audience or adding print and audio mediums to an existing digital book.

> You want to avoid an overreliance on any one revenue source, just like you want to avoid an overreliance on any one traffic source

3. Go **deeper** on an existing revenue source. For instance, adding a coaching arm to a successful digital product line in your business. Adding monthly retainers or value-based pricing which allow you to price based on the return on investment (ROI) you get for your client versus billing an hourly rate. Or adding events to your coaching business to create a transformational and intimate experience for your ideal customer.

But before we do this, it's important to identify what sources and types of revenue you currently have.

Is all revenue good revenue? Not quite.

Good revenue is derived from our zone of genius. These are offers and programs where we can get the best results for our customers.

Bad revenue is derived from work that doesn't allow us to give our customers the greatest transformation possible. This revenue is derived not from our zone of genius but just because we wanted business. It may also require a large amount of resources to fulfill. Remember we spoke about negative personas or people who are not right for your business? Bad revenue could also be sources where you serve your negative persona but don't want to. If we had a choice, it's these revenue channels that we would love to cull but yet stick with out of necessity—just to get business.

In the space below, list out all the revenue sources you have. Try to get as detailed as you can and pull out your figures from the Your Offers section. For example, list out each digital product you sell, the number of copies you sold, refunds if any, and how much money each product made.

REVENUE EARNED IN PREVIOUS YEAR

List out all your business expenses. Break them down into annual and recurring payments.

Recurring Payment   **Annual Payment**

**EXPENSES FOR
THE PREVIOUS YEAR**

TOTAL ANNUAL REVENUE: ···

TOTAL ANNUAL EXPENSES: ···

TAXES PAID: ···

Did you meet your previous annual revenue goals? How much did you exceed your goal by or how much were you short?

Are there any "eggs all in one basket" situations in your business? I.e., an overreliance on one source of revenue?

What hurdles did you have with specific revenue sources? I.e., which ones did you struggle the most with and why?

Is your primary business model aligned with your zone of genius? I.e., your business model is how your business intends to operate and make money.

What revenue sources are not within your zone of genius (which you don't enjoy and would cull if you had the option to)?

Are your current offers (services & products) due for a raise in rates or prices? How could you provide more value for your clients to convince them to pay your new rates or prices?

List all the ways you could go wider on each income source. You are not validating or judging your ideas here. You are just listing every possible idea that comes to your mind.

Revenue Source	Ideas to go wider (e.g., repurpose to a different market or platform)

CREATE An Intensive Biz Playbook & Planner For Solopreneurs

List all the ways you could go deeper into each income source. Again, approach this exercise with no blinders on.

Revenue Source	Ideas to go deeper (adding an additional arm, more access, etc.)

What new revenue streams can you add to your business? E.g., self-publishing, physical product, etc.

Leave blank if you need to.

CREATE An Intensive Biz Playbook & Planner For Solopreneurs

What revenue goal do you want to hit in the next year?

ANNUAL REVENUE GOAL: ....

STRETCH GOAL: ....

TOTAL ESTIMATED EXPENSES PER YEAR: ....

ESTIMATED TAXES: ....

Plan of action to meet that goal

INCOME PLAN

Income Source	Price of Item	Copies Sold	Estimated Monthly Sales	Duration (How many months)	Predicted Yearly Income
Evergreen Products					
Total Predicted Revenue					
Active Launches & Sales Promotions					
Total Predicted Revenue					
Affiliate Promotions					

Income Source	Price of Item	Copies Sold	Estimated Monthly Sales	Duration (How many months)	Predicted Yearly Income
Service/Coaching Packages					
Total Predicted Revenue					
New Income Sources					
Total Predicted Revenue					
TOTAL PREDICTED REVENUE FOR THE YEAR					
TOTAL PREDICTED EXPENSES					
PROFIT/TAKE-HOME					

YOUR
GOALS

"

There's nothing wrong with staying small. You can do big things with a small team.

CJASON FRIED

Founder & CEO of Basecamp

BIG PICTURE GOALS

List your top three big picture goals for the year as well as 3–5 strategic milestones for each of those goals. These milestones will keep your big picture goals grounded and within reach so that they aren't overwhelming.

Note: For each goal or tactic, be specific about what that looks like. You will not "pitch more podcasts," but you will "pitch four podcasts a month." You will not "increase your income," but you will "earn 100k in the next twelve months." Each goal should be broken down into an execution plan or set of tactics that are measurable and that you can execute. These tactics should have a deadline attached to them. They should also start with an action word—e.g., call, write, conduct, do, join, etc.

Here's an example:

BIG PICTURE GOAL: Earn 200K this year

PLAN OF ACTION:
Estimated 17K a month needed to meet that goal
Current Revenue–12K (Short 5K per month to reach intended goal)
How can you make up the shortfall in revenue? Increase prices/create additional income sources or offers

3–5 STRATEGIC MILESTONES
- Publish first Amazon book by March
- Publish second Amazon book by September
- Create summer school coaching program for May
- Add brainstorm and strategic insight coaching intensives page to website by June

Big Picture Goal 1:

Plan of Action

Strategic Milestones	Due Date/Due Week

Big Picture Goal 2:

Plan of Action

Strategic Milestones	Due Date/Due Week

Big Picture Goal 1:	
Plan of Action	
Strategic Milestones	**Due Date/Due Week**

How will these goals translate into the next four quarters? Let's focus on the first quarter or twelve weeks.

State your twelve-week or first quarter goals:

1.

2.

3.

Break each goal into specific tasks and dates of delivery.

Goal 1:	
Tactics	**Due Date/Due Week**

Goal 2:

Tactics	Due Date/Due Week

CREATE An Intensive Biz Playbook & Planner For Solopreneurs

Goal 3:

Tactics	Due Date/Due Week

YOUR CREATE SPACE

CONCLUSION

"

Timing, perseverance, and ten years of trying will eventually make you look like an overnight success.

BIZ STONE

Cofounder of Twitter

YOU'VE MADE IT TO THE END!

By now, this playbook should be brimming with your creative thoughts, ideas, and scribbles.

My intention with this playbook is to help you open up to the possibilities of what you could do with your business and leave you feeling inspired.

It won't be easy, and every stage of business brings with it new fears, challenges, and limiting beliefs.

Most of these fears and limiting beliefs center around the core areas of selling, buying, and judging your worth as a trusted expert. It's these areas that plagued me as well. In this section, I share with you some of the thought processes that have helped me outgrow these limiting beliefs and fears.

ON BUYING...

Your audience—your ideal customers—are not passive.

The way they buy has changed...

The way they engage with brands has changed...

Heck, even marketing has changed.

As online businesses, we're not just creating content to "make" the sale. We're also creating content to engage and turn readers into subscribers.

Marketers used to be able to pinpoint with accuracy how potential customers learned about their business and products. They were then able to outline when exactly a visitor would become a lead, or as they call it, a prospect, and then a buyer.

That's because consumers didn't have much information on hand to help with their buying decisions. They also had very limited control over how they engaged with a brand.

Now though, your potential customers control how they want to engage with you and when.

They may unsubscribe. They shop around because they have a wealth of information at their fingertips.

The buying process is nonlinear and chaotic.

You can't say with any bit of certainty that Person A will buy your product right after email seven.

You can only optimize your emails, attract the right people, and hope for the best.

Even if everything is right, Person A might not buy at that point in time.

That's the reality of today.

What you can do though is to continue to be top of mind...

I recently had someone read my emails and blog for one whole year before he decided to buy one of my courses. That was an entire year of putting out content and interacting with him with no direct ROI. So a no to your offer right now may not be a no forever.

Continue to send content and engage with your audience so that when they are indeed ready to buy, they come to you first.

ON SELLING...

To sell is to provide value.

Value doesn't necessarily mean free cheat sheets or guides or tips.

Value means busting their myths and mistakes and helping them see where they need to change and how they could change.

Selling gets a bad rep. But if you think about it...we're always selling to our audience in one form or the other.

You're trying to sell them on buying into your thoughts and ideas...on why something is important...on why they should rethink a strategy…on why they should try something.

If you're in business, you're selling.

The sooner you convince yourself of this, the better.

ON CONTENT...

Content is king. But just having content alone will not help you build a profitable business. Here are the mistakes most solopreneurs and small business owners (maybe even you) are making with content.

Mistake #1 Your content doesn't support your marketing goals

Your content has no purpose and is all over the place. It doesn't help position your business in any way or show your authority on the subject of your products or services.

Mistake #2 You think content is only sales content

You show up with content only when it's time for selling.

That type of content is good and necessary, but it only helps a small group of your audience who are ready to buy. What about the 98% who are not ready? They need to be nurtured by your content so that you remain top of mind when they are ready to buy.

Mistake #3 Your content doesn't nudge your audience

The role of content is to take them from stranger to brand advocate. Most businesses only have one type of content and sorely miss pieces from other areas. If you miss content in any one particular area, you're digging a huge hole such that your ideal customer can't continue on to the next stage. The closer they are to decision, the more likely they are to do business with you. I talk more about this in my book *The One Hour Content Plan as well in Your First 100.*

Mistake #4 Your fail the litmus test

This isn't so much a mistake as it is an oversight. The litmus test is something I picked up from Joe Pulizzi's book *Epic Content Marketing*.[11] If your content was erased from the face of the internet, would it leave a gap? Would your target audience miss it?

If your answer is no, then you have work to do. Not all your content pieces will be stellar, but you should set the bar high and aim to stand out among businesses who serve a similar audience as yours does.

Mistake #5 You're busy correcting the symptom NOT the real problem

Most people say they're struggling to come up with content ideas. That's just a symptom of larger issues at hand. It shows that you don't have a deeper understanding of the type of content that'll actually help your business. If all of your business comes from one type of work, one type of client, and through one type of marketing, you're taking a big risk. If one client disappears, one social media platform changes its algorithms, or one source of income dries up, you're starting from scratch every time.

ON BEING AN EXPERT...

But, I'm not an expert...

If you've ever wondered that, you need to know that no one starts off as an expert.

An expert isn't someone who has all the right answers.

An expert is someone who is willing to present alternative viewpoints and pose questions to her audience.

An expert is someone willing to dig deep and search for other ways when the current one isn't working. She is willing to go against the grain and challenge the norms even if everyone is doing it that way.

An expert is someone who is willing to answer "it depends" to a yes or no question.

Because it depends is a valid answer.

When you pick up your copy of this playbook next year, I hope you look back at all the goals you achieved, offers you created, and dreams you dared to dream and bring to light.

I can't wait to see what you create and I'm rooting for you!

Good luck and thank you for sharing your work with the world!

Before you go, remember to download your bonuses at **CREATEPLANNER.COM/WORKBOOK-BONUS.**

I really appreciate your feedback, and I love hearing what you have to say.

Could you leave me a review on Amazon letting me know what you thought of this playbook?

About The Author

Meera Kothand is an email marketing strategist and Amazon best-selling author of the books *The One Hour Content Plan and Your First 100.* Her goal is to make powerful marketing strategies simple and relatable so that solopreneurs and small business owners can build a tribe that's addicted to their zone of genius. She has been featured on Smart Blogger, MarketingProfs, YFS Magazine, Addicted2Success, and several other sites.

Connect with Meera @meerakothand or find her at her slice of the internet: https://www.meerakothand.com.

OTHER BOOKS ON AMAZON

 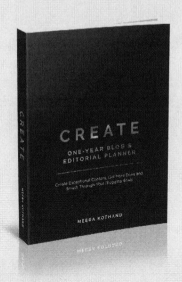 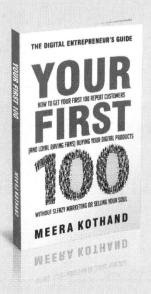

RESOURCES

1. Jeff Ernst quote, "Thought Leadership: How to Achieve the Holy Grail of Content Marketing," *Top Rank Marketing,* December 4, 2014, https://www.toprankmarketing.com/newsroom/guide-to-thought-leadership/

2. Steven Pressfield, *The War of Art: Break Through the Blocks and Win Your Inner Creative Battles,* New York: Black Irish Entertainment, 2012, https://www.amazon.com/War-Art-Through-Creative-Battles/dp/1936891026

3. "What is a Vision Board?" *Make a Vision Board,* https://www.makeavisionboard.com/what-is-a-vision-board/

4. Tom Peters, The Brand You 50 (Reinventing Work): *Fifty Ways to Transform Yourself from an 'Employee' into a Brand That Shouts Distinction, Commitment, and Passion!,* New York: Alfred A. Knopf, 1999, https://www.amazon.com/Brand-You-Transform-Distinction-Commitment/dp/0375407723

5. Tim Ferriss, "Fear Setting: The Most Valuable Exercise I Do Every Month," *Tim,* May 15, 2017, https://tim.blog/2017/05/15/fear-setting/

6. David Finkel, "Escaping the Feast or Famine Cycle: How to Get Your Service Business Past this Recurring Plateau and on the Path to Truly Scale," *Inc.,* November 23, 2016, https://www.inc.com/david-finkel/escaping-the-feast-or-famine-cycle-how-to-get-your-service-business-past-this-re.html

7. "Five-Second Testing," *Usability Hub,* https://usabilityhub.com/guides/five-second-testing

8. Jacob Neilson, "How Long Do Users Stay on Web Pages?", *Neilson Norman Group,* September 12, 2011, https://www.nngroup.com/articles/how-long-do-users-stay-on-web-pages/

9. Donald Miller, *Building a StoryBrand: Clarify Your Message So Customers Will Listen, Nashvill:* HarperCollins Leadership, 2017, https://www.amazon.com/Building-StoryBrand-Clarify-Message-Customers/dp/0718033329

10. Joel Block, *Stop Hustling Gigs and Start Building a Business: 101+ Tricks of the Trade to Help Entrepreneurs and Self-Employed People Build a Money-Making Machine,* California: Bullseye Capital, 2017, https://www.amazon.com/Stop-Hustling-Start-Building-Business/dp/0998934100

11. Joe Pulizzi, Epic Content Marketing: *How to Tell a Different Story, Break through the Clutter, and Win More Customers by Marketing Less,* New York: McGraw-Hill Education, 2013, https://www.amazon.com/Epic-Content-Marketing-Different-Customers/dp/0071819894

Printed in Great Britain
by Amazon